SENTRY

SENTRY

poetry

Tom McSorley

ELBORO

SENTRY Copyright © 2025 by Tom McSorley

All rights reserved. No part of this book may be used or reproduced in any manner whatsoever without written permission except in the case of brief quotations embodied in critical articles and reviews.

Epigraph from *The Watch That Ends the Night*, by Hugh MacLennan, used with permission from McGill-Queen's University Press.

ISBN: 978-1-7379274-9-5

Published in New York City by Elboro Press

Elboro Press books may be purchased in bulk for educational, business or sales promotional use. Please address enquires to:

office@elboropress.com

Elboro Press

First Edition, 2025 – First Printing

Contents

Counting Lesson	3
This Digital Age	5
To My Aunt Veronica in Skyline Acres	7
You Know Wood Never Dies	9
From This Rooftop	11
My Wife Has a Meeting	13
Another Happy Hour	15
Connection	17
Some Truth in the Air?	19
Elsewhere	21
That Old New Year	23
A Vagabonding Boy	25
Haiku: Modern Travel	27
A Century of Aprils	29
Write What You See, Part II	31
Times of Your Life	33
Altitude and Attitude	35
Realization	37
Standards	39
More Steam Room Internationalism	41
Italy-Italia	43
Temporary Assessments	45
Time Periphery	47
Seeker	49
Map of Chicago	51
Haiku: Café NYC	53
Los Alamos	55
Admission	57
Words Become Deeds	59
Birdpoem	61
Shape Maker	63
He Raged	65
Department Store Coffee Break	67
A Coming of Spring	69
Borders of Zoom	71
Virus Vignette	73
The Basements of Spruce Street	75

Love's Expanding Lexicon	77
Sonnet Attempt #2: On His Parents	79
Inspirations	81
Same Old Same Old	83
Unblocking	85
Haiku: Aviation	87
Summer Frame of Mind	89
At Last: Growing Up with Them	91
Another Shakespearean Lesson	93
Sunday Once Again	95
Seawall Sighting	97
Background Performer	99
Café Shards	101
First Sunday After Bobby	103
Summer Tuesday Sketch	105
At Oresti's Taverna, Amsterdam	107
A Fact's a Fact	109
Get Over Yourself	111
Through the Air	113
Reflection	115
Muscle Memory	117
Harbingers	119
One September Morning	121
To Us in the Sistine Chapel	123
What Would Cavafy Do?	125

"…there is no simple explanation for anything important any of us do…"

> Hugh MacLennan
> *The Watch That Ends the Night*

Sentry

COUNTING LESSON

A friend—
an acquaintance—
told me about two
levels of infinity:
countable
and
uncountable;
between those
numbers we can count
forever
lie
more numbers we can count
forever.

He then drew
an
analogy
between
numbers and
words.

I listened,
trying to
decipher
each space
between
each word
he said
and
did not,
could never,
say.

THIS DIGITAL AGE

'Things may fade
at any time
without warning—
we always face
inconsistent
security
architecture—
always and
everywhere,'
a voice from the podium

>   says
>   into
>   my

shapely ears of flesh,
which have taken
to sprouting hair
and swaddling
sounds of this world
in a flannel of advancing age,
as if to hold me in an
impermanent embrace of
soft, somehow secure
semi-silence.

TO MY AUNT VERONICA IN SKYLINE ACRES

Out that window
over the old suburban lawn
seen through the square picture window
in a house where you moved from downtown
with your mother and father
who died lifetimes ago
in spite of your not wanting them to
and your longing for their return.

Out that window
brittle from eyes pounding against it
you can see sometimes
long stilled cars turning into the cracked driveway
to discharge the living and the dead
the ghosts who look down from family portraits
on the wall and stare happily from photo albums
kicking at memory's birth.

YOU KNOW WOOD NEVER DIES

This wooden desk,
a silent refugee
from old sadnesses,
awaits stroking by other pens,
caresses of a softer history
in a new place
where it looks around
at its paper cousins,
loosely arrayed sentries:

Shakespeare, Orwell, Beckett,
Woolf, Marlowe, Faulkner, Nowlan,
Dostoevsky, De Assis, Garcia Marquez.

Just over their shoulders,
out beyond the clear pane
a solitary tree in the
rock garden peers in,
prompted by winds it
firmly twists a welcome
out of the arms of
fresh air brightening.

FROM THIS ROOFTOP

On this roof your eyes
are weary from the heights they have
climbed in search of some clear vision:
maybe they have looked too hard this way
and not enough that — you never know.

There is chaos becoming visible,
loss is settling into view,
but this will not blind you,
as your tired eyes wondrous
will not be shut.

You know you never know:
you know this roof is only so high,
you know people will die,
because you see from above
and from below.

MY WIFE HAS A MEETING

You sit over there
with the woman from Paris.
I sit over here
with the taste of chocolate and coffee.

Although she is facing me,
the woman from Paris does not know
that that man writing something
at the far table
is deeply entwined in the hair
and thought of the woman
she is meeting from Canada
now smiling and speaking
with her back to him,

that man over there
writing something
alone
at the other table.

ANOTHER HAPPY HOUR

Prosecco felt good in their mouths—
even saying the word took them somewhere

beyond a workaday usual:
with its humble bubbles (this is not arrogant champagne)
comes unfamiliar excitement
tentative new sophistication
intimations of change

and giddy possibilities
of possibility.

CONNECTION

Falling asleep,
you stroke
my back.

Rain falls
on a
vacant campsite.

Your fingers are slowing down,
stopping, finally, as you
expire.

Outside, faded signs
wet and aged,
organize empty fields.

SOME TRUTH IN THE AIR?

Lone naked vine in winter
dangles from evergreen
cedar arms
monitoring January
afternoon winds

like a polygraph needle

jumping scratching over
graph paper in some
search for outlines
of truth.

ELSEWHERE

Gray metal

table

shivers
solitary

under

thick layering
crowns

of
snow.

THAT OLD NEW YEAR

We danced with the new year
in Montréal under
dark relentless rain
that went about its anonymous
business of melting dirty urban snow
into opaque puddle mirrors.

Prosecco flowed out of cold night air
into our warm hunger for renewal
under Leonard's surveillance from his stillness
up there buried in Mount Royal,
and we imagine his approval of
our romantic rebellion against this damp
frigid night in an empty park's gazebo

as that inscrutable massive gray
St. Lawrence River churns the ice
gathered on its shorelines to slush,
shoving it down its infinite
spiralling flow of time, reminding us
now to return to our dancing.

A VAGABONDING BOY
(for Phil Tetrault)

Crossing atop Mount Royal
along a curving road
named after an old
corrupt Montréal mayor,
city lights unfurl in four
directions down below
in the late December
early evening.

Where did that gifted
poet live (all reports say
he was of genius intelligence
with schizophrenia) on this
mountain winter and summer?
What did he observe over all
those days and nights; what
did Montréal whisper to him?

He is gone now, as many poets
of the city are, but others are
no doubt spiriting through these
trees looking down this mountain
on what they cannot contain in
themselves, in others, and are
poised to wreath this holy
topography with their own hymns.

HAIKU: MODERN TRAVEL

Snowy train's wake blur
swaying landscape dissolving.
We bend to our phones.

A CENTURY OF APRILS
(for Atom Egoyan)

He and she may have thought
    in some stubborn vulnerable
Yerevan twilight:
we will take our futures from
this vortex of ghosts whirling
above beneath through us.

We will head for the start of time
    to ancient beginnings in a
dusty north African city
clamorous distraction
stone shapes pyramidic
and feline;
invisible future powers
shimmering
molecular
divine
astride Nassar's Nile
eternal dreaming;

    to a northern pacific smudge –
sketch of another faded empire clinging
to a cold continent's edge at Mile Zero
(where it ends or where it begins?)
with plush performance at that
Empress Hotel all feigned tea
certainties silently soured by
nearby impermanent exterminations
echoing sadly familiar
over infinite waters
past steadfast Esquimalt watchtowers

under Salish and Haida eyes.

We could not imagine
we would see the lights trimming
this provincial Canadian
government house become
floating baubles upon the harbour
as sea planes furrow dark water
in slack parallel sprays
under groans of
dopplering decelerations
announcing small arrivals
having nothing to do with
all those Aprils in
Armenia.

WRITE WHAT YOU SEE, PART II

Inkwell and lens
on a wooden desk
quietly cohabiting:

one needs a pen;
the other, a camera.

Searches for completion
require patience.

TIMES OF YOUR LIFE

Trying to inscribe
  your colours
   on the air
     is
    one
   ambition;

 recognizing your
   dignified
 disappearance
     is
    quite
   another.

ALTITUDE AND ATTITUDE
(for Patrick)

'It's always sunny
at 35,000 feet,'
my aviator brother would say.

Sitting now
aboard this plane,
I see he is right.

Meanwhile, I carry
those absent clouds and rain
inside me.

REALIZATION

He imagined his
private thoughts
could

become
public inclinations
and sell millions.

He was wrong.

STANDARDS

Beckett
would have
reconsidered

—even stroked out—

each of the
words I have
just written.

MORE STEAM ROOM INTERNATIONALISM

A sweaty Mandarin badinage
on one bench as these two women
slap parts of their bodies and
chat about what must surely be
infinite mysteries;

across from them, closer to me,
a couple of Haitian matriarchs
sculpt steam into muscular French
javelins filigreed with (I think)
occasional Creole chiselling.

My hot house defined,
me a beige rouge blur inside it,
I remain at rest in
a moist clarified
silence.

ITALY-ITALIA

Old Italian man
small thin gray
haired watches
me pass to and
from the gym.

Occasionally there is
an exchange of nods;
sometimes a young
woman sits with
him, chatting calmly
in Italian.

He looks out at a
street, its passing
cars unceasing,
perhaps conjuring
sounds from his
childhood in Calabria,

when the world stretched
out wide before him
before now
in Little Italy,
Preston Street, Ottawa.

TEMPORARY ASSESSMENTS

Everything you claimed
as significant to yourself,
worthy of inscription, was in order
to identify yourself,
to not pass through
that permeable amnesiac
membrane of time.

This undertaking faces considerable,
if not insurmountable,
obstacles.

As you age, your claims become
more modest now,
informed by an experience of erosion,
a sense that the small stain
of your residue
is all that remains and is
almost enough.

TIME PERIPHERY

Shadow of bird
across a line
of cedars
sketches
the day
into shape:

pay
attention.

SEEKER

A fox on the airfield
                       tail down
snout first under a
chain link barrier,
crossing asphalt to
neighbouring golf course,

searches for wildness.

MAP OF CHICAGO

The Latino chef is waving
a towel and mouthing
words to a song
bouncing barely above
densely packed din of
his restaurant.

Beside us on one side of our table
electrified young Americans
take pictures of their tacos
publishing them instantly
to a Cloud that dreams for them
some secure omniscience.

At the table on our other side
a man tells (loudly) a woman
that he brings emotional
maturity to those around him,
and can honestly say he's helped
build the company and has no regrets.

It is here in Chicago
where we overhear—
across state lines of Mexican tapas
and Oregon Pinot Noir—
intimations of something's end
or the origins of something else.

HAIKU: CAFÉ NYC

Aimless heart alone
Fear of not being enough
Waitress preparing

LOS ALAMOS

On high sad mesas
we learned how to kill
massively, secretively;
a project of death
calculated calibrated—

designed to melt ancient Aztec
stone and vaporize the flesh
of now and forever.

A winding road up
to the flat top expanses
of some barren eternity,
a closely watched
asphalt ribbon of terror.

ADMISSION
(for Leonard Cohen)

Others are blessed
with a flow, an aged
poet said.

I am one of the ones,
he continued,
who is not.

WORDS BECOME DEEDS
(for David Adams Richards on his 70th birthday)

In the stubborn
stinking drunken
poverty of it, he continued
word upon word
to write a map
of his awareness,
his suffering,
his love, and his
doubt that saved
this place he saw
disappearing, wrongly:

a human place
filled with cruelty and failure
and goodness and mercy
and humility; like
Dickens and Dostoevsky,
Hardy and Tolstoy,
he perceived and
he witnessed,
and wrote unafraid
that life itself
is here, too.

BIRDPOEM
(for William Carlos Williams)

small bird
upon brown speckled
snowbank

pecking winter
to its slow
melting death

cheers me with
its humble
monumental

drama of
unwitting
affirmation

SHAPE MAKER
(for Alden Nowlan)

Atop tiny shoulders
his bulky head,

with broad bright
face twinkling,

folds infinities
of experience into

a vast origami of
expression.

HE RAGED

All the world's leaf blowers
must be dismantled,
shipped immediately to
the malicious miscreant
who conjured this infernal
machine; this inventive person
must henceforth in perpetuity
sit in silence amongst
the millions of stilled parts
as penance for crimes
against the audible world.

DEPARTMENT STORE COFFEE BREAK

The women toss their hair
warming the air
between them
all sitting and too loud talking
all smiles and aimless looking
preening for no one,
for everyone;
forgiving themselves,
each other and that
relentless human traffic
before daubing lips
and getting back
to the towels
to the bedding
to the appliances
to the fragrances
and the lotions
that join them
in the struggle
to keep beauty
alive
here
and
everywhere.

A COMING OF SPRING

Cardinal red
against
slate gray
sky

green tree
backdrop
yields to
final snow

fragments
drifting
down
out of winter

BORDERS OF ZOOM

Waiting to join
waiting for admission
waiting for one's turn
to speak out of one's
screen rectangle;

waiting for borderless
air to again wrap our shapes
and sounds in
formless joyful elusive
interaction.

VIRUS VIGNETTE

Wine glass on a history of Latin America,
silent JBL speakers staring me down.

"Okay, now we're going to sign off:
I love you all." I hear my wife speak
into her computer screen.

The cat glides by my feet,
headed elsewhere, nowhere.

Outside, a virus seeks to
stitch itself into every
space between us.

THE BASEMENTS OF SPRUCE STREET

In concrete sinks
eels swim in darkness;

silverfish squadrons
patrol empires of spiders;

ancient tree roots
strain to push up through
dank concrete floors;

the basements of Spruce Street
should be visited only infrequently,
always on high alert.

LOVE'S EXPANDING LEXICON

The description of the wine
read 'nutty complexity' and

'bracing acidity;' quite
unintentionally capturing

at least two essences of
his beloved wife.

He mentions this to her
and she smiles.

SONNET ATTEMPT #2: ON HIS PARENTS

He felt somehow his life could not go on
and yet it did in ways he cannot stop;
watched strange and loose actions gather at dawn
remove or hold those tears about to drop.

It was something about those gone away,
so missed so dear so far and yet so here
that bade him see colours beyond mere gray,
a way out of sadness and useless fear.

They brought this world for him to try to build
up by and for himself in his fashion,
loving and hoping he would be fulfilled
while he would try every style of passion.

His melancholy transformed by such gifts,
now love and kindness brush his wings and lift.

INSPIRATIONS

Windmills of Wolfe Island
are turning turning turning
in their stark sparse swirl forest

snatching electricity from invisible restless air
that used to merely breeze
over water and land unsigned

on its way nowhere
to the American southern
shores of Lake Ontario.

SAME OLD SAME OLD

Say it another way, if you can.

Oblique angles, eccentric
evocations, odd insinuations
are of interest,
not all this literal
'see what I mean?'

If you're worried about growing old,
for instance, mention that ghosts now gather
under fluorescent lights,
dart away around hallway corners,
scatter mercurial in your blood
and memory.

Still too obvious, but you get the idea.

UNBLOCKING

You don't have
to write anything,
you can just sit
there silently.

At last, he was grateful
for this new space
a blank page
gave him.

HAIKU: AVIATION

  fractal birds scatter
the sheer size of that vast sky
    I look to ascend

SUMMER FRAME OF MIND

pale sheeting rains
shoulders tensed in resistance
dutiful umbrella protests
July disappointment

fugitive summer
children watch out
windows hoping
skies will clear

pools will open
and flickering
thoughts of classrooms
will not gather

AT LAST: GROWING UP WITH THEM

Years later, they still gathered at
their old riverbanks
saying, 'look, the flow, the flow!'

he knew what they meant,
that they were right:
he returned their smiles

and their waving
from what he used to
think was the other side.

ANOTHER SHAKESPEAREAN LESSON

He recalls how arrogant Hotspur
claimed he could call to his side
all-powerful gods and wizards

and remembers too his rival
Prince Hal's response:
yes, you can call them,
but will they show up?

In this he hears
an intimation of how
he goes through life in a similar tangle
of confidence and doubt.

SUNDAY ONCE AGAIN

Snow squalls.

A crazed neighbour screams
her anger at her lover
over their inert wan yard.

Winter winds make
light bulbs shiver

your old Sunday night
sadness

is not exactly helped by this
stunningly morose Icelandic band;
but you listen anyway,

thinking,

tomorrow I can manage
these dark distances again

if the sun rises
if skies clear.

SEAWALL SIGHTING

Heron
hunches
waiting

at
ocean
edges
pocked
by
rains:

the bird
does not
know
it is
a
bird.

BACKGROUND PERFORMER

Under skies draining:
the hunger, the waiting

to embody the background
of someone else's vision.

A lingering, and then
you're not needed.

Blunt return to
real periphery,

from background
to oblivion

on a diluvial
New York afternoon.

CAFÉ SHARDS

Roar of water below
my lonely afternoon
terrace table
distant pulsing bass line
from somewhere

white pigeon lands on
ancient hewn stone

fishers discard empty beer
cans to resume their
search through that
filthy Roman
canal

the homely waitress has
a winning smile and sexy legs
heavyset Germans arrive
to order drinks in
clotted French

   the magic of solitude is wearing thin

as two women with suitcases
amble away,
the waitress cries
"Bye bye les filles"

I resist the urge to take pictures
I am not sure why

FIRST SUNDAY AFTER BOBBY
(for Robert Gallie, 1940-2024)

Winds move along
pushing stray sky from
somewhere to somewhere
else

a few hours from here and
far from now his family will toast
a life that he led until
yesterday—

I have no doubt that open sky where they are
will offer this same obscure
transference of energy invisible,
here

and then gone.

SUMMER TUESDAY SKETCH

  Wine glass upon a balcony
     as aspiring de Chirico
    street drawn below
    yawns and meanders
  stretching out louche lean
      for the coming
        of night.

He watches those wandering
    up inclining asphalt
  to a pub at the top; they
  sometimes glance at him,
his wine glass, his slow smile,
his "I'm not going anywhere"
      je ne sais quoi.

AT ORESTI'S TAVERNA, AMSTERDAM

I sit alone
at this taverna:

others observe
me with
compassion,
imagining my
world of
solitude
and, perhaps,
dignity.

When my
companion
arrives,
I
wonder if
they will
look at me
differently.

Which version
would I prefer?

A FACT'S A FACT

Loons slaughter
ducklings:

on mirror lake
surfaces
under blue skies
and oceans of
stars

nature's riot
of murder
and copulation
has no
time

for our empathy
our kindness
or, least of all,

our
poetry.

GET OVER YOURSELF

The cosmic spatial temporal
   argument lost,

he turns his attention to that
   street below

keening alive with dogs and children
   awaiting the coming snow.

THROUGH THE AIR

Murmuration of
      dragonflies
surprise the
      evening

      as we try to
  remember bird names
accustomed to such
        aerial activity

REFLECTION

He wants to rush
to the end;
sometimes his pen
won't let him,
even succeeding
occasionally to get
him to
turn back.

MUSCLE MEMORY

Tapping familiar drum
patterns with his fingers
gave him
solace:

a peculiar interior
metronome of control,
of devotion to
structures of rhythm

imprinted on him
and related to his
tempo of
being

as if arrived at
by chance
but really not
at all—

more like a frenetic collage
Morse Code variant saying who he was,
writing in sand,
"I am here."

HARBINGERS

Beaming big
wafer moon
clear sky
illuminated

you play
backgammon
on your phone
as we look up

a sepia moonlit
cast over the
declining flowers
as autumn arrives

ONE SEPTEMBER MORNING

That solitary cloud
looks like your eyebrow,
you say:

to me it seems rather
a folded gossamer
paper on a
diffuse Magritte canvas;

whatever it is
as it drifts
across a morning sky
this limpid faraway
condensation
speaks of the metaphor
of me and you—

how differently
we see
and
how we yearn
to see

together.

TO US IN THE SISTINE CHAPEL
(for Tina and for my children)

All those myths
of our creation scoured
out of air and terra firma
and earthly pigment
across dour centuries:
such illuminations dimming in
shadows of doubt, lacerations of reason.

Looking up now
it seems so insubstantial,
a helpless human idea
dreaming itself into
being on rough stone
walls and ceilings,
wishing that celestial
finger would touch you,
me, all of us
waiting below;
but knowing as we
filter through these chambers
that such a wish was
designed to be nothing more
than the continuation of
such a wish.

Quietly now we exit,
holding hands together
gently in the gathering
throngs about to disperse
into the piazza, the streets,
and those rivers of time
endless and only ours.

WHAT WOULD CAVAFY DO?

Smiling slowly at
his soundless
longing,

while a blue mirror of sea
is brushed with streaks of white
by distant winds
only now exhausting themselves
on edges of blank papers
he has

assembled on a small black table
upon which he is
about to write.

www.ingramcontent.com/pod-product-compliance
Lightning Source LLC
Chambersburg PA
CBHW071856070526
44583CB00016B/1710